Washington's Birthday

Dennis Brindell Fradin

—Best Holiday Books—

ENSLOW PUBLISHERS, INC.
Bloy St. & Ramsey Ave.   P.O. Box 38
Box 777   Aldershot
Hillside, N.J. 07205   Hants GU12 6BP
U.S.A.   U.K.

For my lovely sister, Lori Fradin

Library of Congress Cataloging-in-Publication Data

Fradin, Dennis B.
    Washington's Birthday / by Dennis Brindell Fradin.
        p. cm.—(Best holiday books)
    Includes index.
    Summary: Discusses how the achievements of our nation's first president led to
the present-day celebration of his birth.
    ISBN 0-89490-235-0
    1. Washington's Birthday—Juvenile literature. 2. Washington, George,
1732-1799—Juvenile literature. [1. Washington's Birthday. 2. Washington,
George, 1732-1799.] I. Title. II. Series: Fradin, Dennis B. Best holiday books.
E312.6.F83 1990
973.4'1'092—dc20
    [B]   89-7664
                                      CIP

48p. illus

                                      AC

Printed in the United States of America

10 9 8 7 6 5 4 3 2 1

Illustration Credits:
Cameramann International, Ltd.: p. 40; Currier & Ives, Birthplace of Washington,
Museum of the City of New York: p. 29; Tom Dunnington: p. 12; General Research
Division, The New York Public Library, Astor, Lenox, and Tilden Foundation: p. 15;
Library of Congress: pp. 7, 17, 19, 21, 22, 24, 25, 32, 35, 43, 44; Courtesy of The
Mount Vernon Ladies' Association: pp. 8, 9; National Portrait Gallery, Smithsonian
Institution, Washington, D.C.: pp. 4, 14, 28.

Cover Illustration by Charlott Nathan

Contents

Portrait of George Washington, who is called "the Father of Our
Country" because of all that he did for the United States

The Father of Our Country

Who was the most famous person in United States history? Many people would say "George Washington."

Washington led U.S. troops when the country freed itself from England over 200 years ago. A few years later, he became the nation's first president. For all that he did, Washington is called "the Father of Our Country."

George Washington's birthday is a national holiday. We celebrate it on the third Monday in February. All Americans should know at least a little about why we honor Washington's Birthday each year.

The Father of Our Country Was Once Young

George Washington was born in eastern Virginia on February 22, 1732. As a child, George moved with his family several times around eastern Virginia. Along the way, he had some schooling. He learned to read and write, but his best subject was math.

George had a half-brother, Lawrence, who was 14 years older than he. In 1740, when George was eight, Lawrence went off to fight Spain for England. The 13 American colonies were ruled by England, which was called the "mother country." Lawrence Washington was one of many Americans who helped England fight its wars. Two years later, Lawrence returned. Ten-year-old George began thinking about a military life as he listened to Lawrence's war stories.

When George was 11, his father died. George helped his mother raise his three younger brothers and younger sister. He also spent a lot of time at Lawrence's farm, Mount Vernon. Lawrence was more than a half-brother to George. He was like a second father to him.

George was tall and athletic. He loved to ride horses and hunt and fish. By his teens, he loved dancing with young ladies. But he could not earn a living doing any of these things. He and his family wondered: What would he be?

Lawrence thought George should join the English navy. George liked the idea, but his mother had to approve because he was just 14. Mary Washington would not let him join the navy at so young an age.

George was good at math and at making maps. He decided to become a surveyor— someone who figures land boundaries. At 16, he helped survey the Virginia wilderness for the rich Lord Fairfax. On this trip he learned to sleep in the woods, cook over a fire, and cross rivers on his horse. From then on, he felt at home in the wilderness. George bought land with his surveying pay. By the age of 19, he owned about 1,500 acres.

This portrait of Lawrence Washington, George's half-brother, still hangs on a wall at Mount Vernon.

When George neared 20, Lawrence became very sick. Lawrence sailed to the island of Barbados for his health and took George along. George came down with smallpox on Barbados but recovered. Lawrence died soon after sailing home in the summer of 1752. Lawrence's home, Mount Vernon, later went to George.

Mount Vernon, George Washington's famous home, as seen today

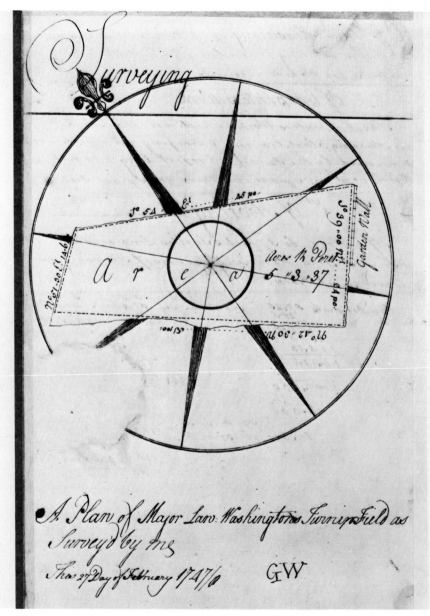

George Washington did this survey of Lawrence Washington's turnip field
when he was just 16 years old.

George Washington Becomes a Soldier

In 1753, France built several forts in western Pennsylvania. The Virginia Colony claimed that region. The governor of Virginia wanted to tell the French to leave.

In the fall of 1753, 21-year-old George Washington offered to carry the message. He set out with six men that November. After about a month in the wilderness, they reached the French commander at Fort Le Boeuf in Pennsylvania. The commander said that France claimed the region and would not leave.

The explorer Christopher Gist made the return trip with Washington. Once, the two of them were crossing the icy Allegheny River on

George Washington in the icy Allegheny River

a raft. Suddenly the raft jerked, spilling Washington into the cold water. He climbed back onto the raft, but the wild water spun it out of control. Luckily, the two men reached an island. During their freezing night on the island, the river froze. In the morning, they walked across the ice to the shore!

Washington reached Virginia's governor in January of 1754. After giving him the French answer, Washington suggested that they build their own fort in southwestern Pennsylvania. The governor sent men to build this fort, which was the start of the city of Pittsburgh, Pennsylvania.

The governor soon sent Washington out with troops to protect the fort. While going there, Washington and his men defeated a French force in southwestern Pennsylvania. This fight, which took place on May 28, 1754, began a big war between England and France. It was called the French and Indian War (1754–1763), because many Indians helped the French.

During this war, Washington became known

A rather young-looking George Washington

as a very good soldier. In July of 1754, he held a fort for a time against great odds before having to give it up. One year later, he fought bravely in a huge battle in southwestern Pennsylvania.

Braddock's troops approaching Fort Duquesne

The English troops should have beaten the smaller French force in this battle. But the French hid behind trees as they fought. They were able to pick off the English soldiers easily. Washington begged the English general, Edward Braddock, to let the men fight like the French. Braddock refused. Like other English generals of the time, he thought it was cowardly to hide during battle.

The English army was crushed in this Battle of the Wilderness, which was fought on July 9, 1755. General Braddock and many of his men were killed. George Washington survived, but two horses were shot out from under him and four bullets pierced his coat, just missing him. Washington prevented an even bigger loss of lives by leading the survivors away.

England later won the French and Indian War. But George Washington's role in it was done by late 1758. He had learned a great deal by then. He knew that the English way of fighting didn't work in the American woods. And he had seen that the English could be beaten.

The French crushed the English forces in the Battle of the Wilderness, which was fought in 1755.

George Washington and the Revolutionary War

In January of 1759 George Washington married Martha Dandridge Custis. Martha was a widow with two children—Jackie (a boy) and Patsy (a girl). George Washington grew to love the children very much.

The family lived at Mount Vernon. For the next 15 years, George Washington farmed and went to balls with Martha. He also served in Virginia's lawmaking body, the House of Burgesses.

Trouble between England and the 13 American colonies began in the 1760s. England needed money to pay for the French and Indian War. The "mother country" decided to raise it by taxing the Americans. The colonists were to pay taxes on many goods from tea to paint.

Thousands of Americans called these taxes unfair and would not pay them. In the fall of 1774 American leaders met in Philadelphia, Pennsylvania, to talk over the tax problem.

George Washington meeting Martha Custis and her two children, Jackie and Patsy

George Washington was one of seven Virginians sent to this First Continental Congress. The other American leaders viewed him as a quiet, strong man of good judgment.

The First Continental Congress could not get England to act more fairly. On April 19, 1775, war began between England and the Americans. It was called the Revolutionary War (1775–1783). The 13 colonies—which soon called themselves the United States—fought it to become independent of England.

Three weeks after the war started, a second big meeting of American leaders opened in Philadelphia. It was called the Second Continental Congress. George Washington wanted to show that he was ready to fight. He wore his French and Indian War uniform to Congress.

The Americans needed an army and someone to command it. On June 14, 1775, Congress formed the Continental Army, the forerunner of the U.S. Army. George Washington had the most war experience among well-known

Americans. Congress elected him leader of the army on June 15.

Washington took command of the army on July 3, 1775, in Massachusetts. He found the army in a very bad state. The supply of gunpowder was very low. Some of the men had old

After the Battle of Concord (Massachusetts), the Americans hid behind walls and fences and fired on the retreating British.

weapons that did not fire. Many soldiers would not follow orders. And some went home whenever they felt like it.

Early in the war, Washington saw that his troops were not yet ready for big battles.

George Washington taking command of the Continental Army at Cambridge, Massachusetts, on July 3, 1775

Instead, he mostly fought small battles while training his men. The Americans won some of these battles. For several years, though, it looked as though they would lose the war.

The winter of 1777–1778 was the low point for the Americans. Washington and his 11,000 cold, sick, and hungry men spent that winter at Valley Forge, Pennsylvania. Although Martha Washington and other wives came to nurse the sick, 3,000 men died at Valley Forge. Many of the survivors were ready to give up, but George Washington convinced them that they could still win the war.

Meanwhile, some American lawmakers and some military men were saying that Washington was a bad general. They thought he should be making big attacks. They didn't understand that the English might have crushed the Revolution had Washington tried it.

Washington rarely lost his temper. But he was enraged when he heard what the lawmakers were saying. He sent a letter to the American government in Philadelphia. In it he wrote that the lawmakers in their warm rooms had no idea what war was really like.

In the spring, good news reached Valley Forge. France had joined the Americans' side. French aid turned the tide. Finally, Washington and his forces fought and won a very big battle.

George Washington shared the hardships with his men at Valley Forge.

During the Revolutionary War, Washington often entered the thick of the fighting. Here he is encouraging his men at the Battle of Princeton (New Jersey) in early 1777.

Called the Battle of Yorktown, it was fought in Virginia in October of 1781. A huge British army surrendered after this battle.

The Battle of Yorktown marked the end of major fighting. The Americans had won the Revolutionary War. The United States stood on its own, free of England!

The New Country's Most Famous Person

George Washington was a living legend by the end of the war. People now knew that he had been wise to avoid big battles at first. And they knew that his iron will had made the difference between victory and defeat.

Martha and George Washington had been apart for most of seven years. With the war over, they hoped to live quietly. Their family had suffered tragedy in the past few years. Patsy had died at 17 and Jackie at 27. But Jackie had left four children. Martha and George adopted two of these grandchildren.

The Washingtons could not live quietly. People came to Mount Vernon to look at George

Martha Washington

Washington's home. Some even knocked on the door, hoping to shake his hand. Not wanting to disappoint people, George and Martha entertained many strangers.

Washington was so popular that hundreds of parents named their children for him. Some

Washington's birthplace, as portrayed in a Currier & Ives print

people even wanted Washington to be king of the United States. This upset him. Americans had fought to free themselves from the rule of England's king, he said. The last thing they needed was their own king.

The problem was that the U.S. government was weak. It looked as though the nation might fall apart. In 1787, George Washington headed a big meeting that was held in Philadelphia to strengthen the nation. The laws that American leaders created at this meeting were put into a paper called the United States Constitution. The Constitution has been the law of the land for over 200 years.

Our First President

The Constitution ordered that a president be elected to lead the country. George Washington was easily elected the first president in early 1789. He and Martha went to live in New York City, which was then the U.S. capital. Later they lived in Philadelphia, which became the capital in late 1790.

Washington served two terms as president. He strengthened the nation. He kept it out of war. And he kept the states from fighting each other.

The president was not protected in those days. He walked the streets the same as other people. For exercise, he rode his horse through

George Washington's inauguration as first president took place in New York City on April 30, 1789.

the countryside. George and Martha Washington also held "open houses." Anyone who wanted to meet them could do so.

President Washington had a soft spot for old Revolutionary War soldiers. He liked to talk over the war days with old soldiers who stopped by the President's Mansion. He gave money to old soldiers in need.

Honoring George Washington

After eight years as president, George Washington retired. He and Martha could finally return to Mount Vernon. But less than three years later, George Washington died on December 14, 1799.

Even in death, Washington did something great. Like many other rich Americans, he had owned slaves. But he had turned against slavery in his later years. His will provided that his slaves be freed after Martha's death.

Americans have honored Washington's memory in many ways. A new city replaced Philadelphia as the U.S. capital in 1800. It was

Washington at Mount Vernon just after he retired from the presidency

named Washington, D.C., for our first president. The state of Washington and many towns were also named for him. In addition, George Washington's picture is on U.S. dollar bills and quarters. And each year, millions of Americans celebrate George Washington's birthday.

The Story of George Washington's Birthday

In 1778, at Valley Forge, George Washington's men wanted to show appreciation for him. They played a drum and fife (a flute-like instrument) concert for him on his birthday. This was the first public celebration of Washington's birthday.

Later, big birthday parties were held for President Washington. All four and one-half million people who lived in the United States could not attend! So towns across the nation held their own ceremonies. Cannons were fired in honor of George Washington. Poems and speeches about him were read. Songs about him were sung.

In the first years after Washington's death, the custom of honoring his birthday almost died out. Then came the year 1832, which marked the 100th year since Washington's birth. Big celebrations were held in many places that year. They have been held ever since.

In the 1800s and for most of the 1900s, Washington's Birthday was honored on February 22. Then, the U.S. Congress moved the holiday to the third Monday in February starting in 1971. This was done to give many people a three-day weekend.

President Abraham Lincoln was also born in February. Some states honor both great presidents on the third Monday in February. They call the holiday Presidents' Day.

Schoolchildren and Washington's Birthday

As Washington's Birthday approaches, millions of schoolchildren do special projects. Their teachers read them stories about Washington's life. Then the children write their own stories and poems about him. Some schools hold contests to see who can write the best essay about George Washington. And some schools perform plays about George Washington and the Revolutionary War.

Art projects are also popular school activities. Portraits of George Washington were made during his lifetime, and so we know what he looked like. Many children draw pictures or silhouettes of Washington. A silhouette is an outline of a person's head or body.

These children have cut out silhouettes of George Washington as an art project.

The Third Monday in February

Washington's Birthday is a federal (national) holiday. There is no mail on the third Monday in February. U.S. government offices are closed, as are many schools and businesses.

Hundreds of U.S. cities and towns hold Washington's Birthday ceremonies. These usually include speeches. There may also be parades at which people dress in Revolutionary War uniforms.

Special ceremonies are held at places that were important to George Washington's life. At Mount Vernon, Virginia, there are wreath-laying ceremonies at George Washington's burial site. At Valley Forge, Pennsylvania, scenes from the awful winter the army spent there are enacted during the Washington's birthday weekend.

Among American families, a certain food has long been popular on Washington's birthday. The food is cherry pie. This custom stems from an old story about George Washington. When George was a boy, the story goes, he chopped down a cherry tree. His father asked him what happened to the tree. "I cannot tell a lie, Pa," George supposedly answered. "I did it with my hatchet."

Millions of American children including Abraham Lincoln grew up enjoying this story. But it was made up by an author. The author wanted to show that George was very honest. Thanks to this story, though, baking and eating cherry pies on Washington's Birthday became a custom.

There is no need to make up stories about George Washington's good traits. He had so many of them! Washington was very brave. He was a man of peace, yet he fought when necessary. He was loyal to his friends. He cared deeply about his family. He inspired other people to do well. And he was willing to change his mind—as was shown by his turning against slavery.

These are the qualities about George Washington that we should remember on his birthday. Do you think they are qualities we should try to have, too?

The man whose birthday has been honored for over 200 years

George and Martha Washington at breakfast with their adopted
grandchildren, Eleanor Parke Custis and George Washington Parke Custis

Glossary

capital—the place where laws are made for a nation or state

Continental Army—the forerunner of the U.S. Army

Continental Congress—the forerunner of the U.S. Congress

custom—a way of doing things that people teach their children.

election—an event in which people vote

fife—a flute-like instrument

House of Burgesses—colonial Virginia's law-making body

military—concerning the armed forces

million—a thousand thousand (1,000,000)

president—an important leader; the United States' main leader is called the president

Revolutionary War—the war for independence that the United States fought with Great Britain in 1775-1783

silhouette—an outline of a person's head or body

slavery—the practice of owning people

smallpox—a disease that once killed many people but has been wiped out

surveyor—someone who figures land boundaries

thousand—ten hundred (1,000)

tragedy—something that is very sad

U.S. Constitution—the basic laws of the nation

widow—a woman whose husband is dead

wreath—a round decoration usually made of plants

Index